LONGMAN

PICTURE DICTIONARY

T0385794

Name: _____

Age: _____

Address: _____

_____

_____

_____

_____

_____

JULIE ASHWORTH ■ JOHN CLARK

Pearson Education Limited
Edinburgh Gate
Harlow
Essex
CM20 2JE
England
and associated companies throughout the world

Visit our website: http://www.pearsonELT.com/dictionaries

First published by Nelson ELT 1993

26 25 24 23 22 21
IMP 36 35 34 33 32 31

ISBN 978-0-17-556454-5

Printed in Italy by L.E.G.O. S.p.A. Lavis (TN)
GCC/29

Acknowledgements

The authors would like to thank the following consultants
and teachers for their valuable feedback: Gwyneth Fox, Jackie
Holderness, Wendy Superfine, Denise Werlé.

Design: Julie Ashworth

Photos: Anton Stark at Rodley Studios, Leeds (Tel: 0532
557272).

Illustrations: Julie Ashworth (pages 6, 8, 9, 20, 21, 40, 41, 42,
44, 45, 56, 57, 62); Rowan Barnes-Murphy (pages 24, 36,
37); Jerry Collins (pages 29, 57, 64); Andy Cooke (pages 25,
60, 61); Phil Dobson (pages 34, 46, 47, 48, 49); John Gosler
(page 63); David Parkins (pages 18, 19, 38, 39, 54, 55, 58,
59); Valeria Petrone (52, 53); Marie José Sacré (30, 31, 32,
33); Pippa Sampson (pages 12, 14, 22, 23, 50, 51); Peter
Schrank (pages 11, 28, 29, 30).

Introduction

The Longman Picture Dictionary is specially designed for use in the classroom or at home. It can equally be enjoyed by the child working alone, the child working with a parent/guardian or friend and, of course, the child in class.

The dictionary is divided into two parts. The first part is a full colour picture dictionary. Words are listed alphabetically and grouped according to topic. The second part is a complete alphabetical list of all the words in the dictionary with page references.

How to use this dictionary

To find the meaning of an English word ...

If you want to know what the word *skirt* means, look under the letter *s* in the wordlist at the back of the book. The number next to the word tells you which page the word *skirt* is on.

To find an English word for something ...

If you want to know the English word for an article of clothing (eg. a skirt), look at the Contents (pages 4/5) and find the relevant topic, in this case CLOTHES. Turn to page 20. Look for the picture of a skirt in the wordlist and you will find the English word.

To check the spelling of an English word ...

If you want to know how to spell the word *skirt*, look under the letter *s* in the wordlist or find the word on the appropriate page.

Games and activities

There are games and activities on every double-page spread which help develop skills such as sorting, spelling, counting and matching. These can be done by the child working alone (after being given some initial guidance) or, of course, as classroom activities. The beautiful illustrations with interwoven storylines and visual twists allow the pictures to be used time and time again for a variety of language activities such as storytelling, pairwork etc.

Contents

 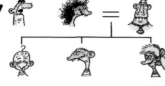

4

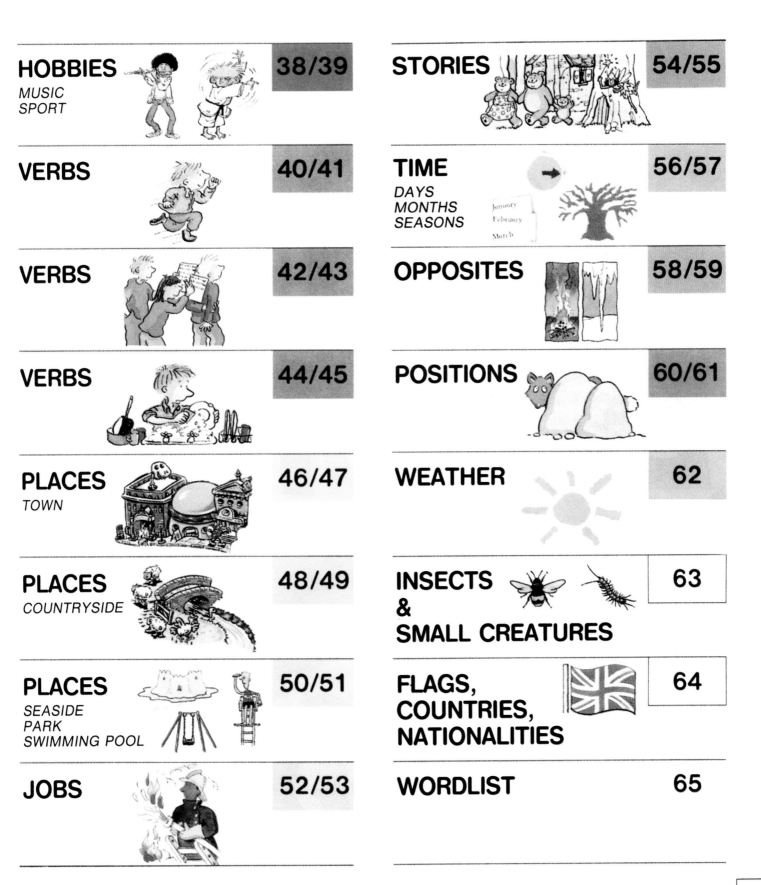

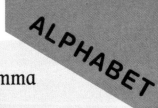

A d E letters
n

B M K capital letters

f j c k small letters

hello goodbye words

PUNCTUATION

, comma

. full stop

? question mark

astronaut	jar	queen
balloon	juggler	rainbow
brush	key	rope
cage	kite	snowman
candle	ladder	suitcase
cobweb	letter	telescope
dinosaur	lobster	tortoise
dustbin	magnet	umbrella
envelope	match	vampire
firework	needle	wheel
flag	newspaper	xylophone
grasshopper	octopus	yacht
hammer	pin	yo-yo
igloo	plaster	zip

- How many letters are there in the alphabet?
- How many words begin with the letter **l**?
- How many letters are there in the word **xylophone**?
- What is the longest word on this page?
- Write these letters in alphabetical order:

  b e i t o n s u y a

- What are these?

7

In Space

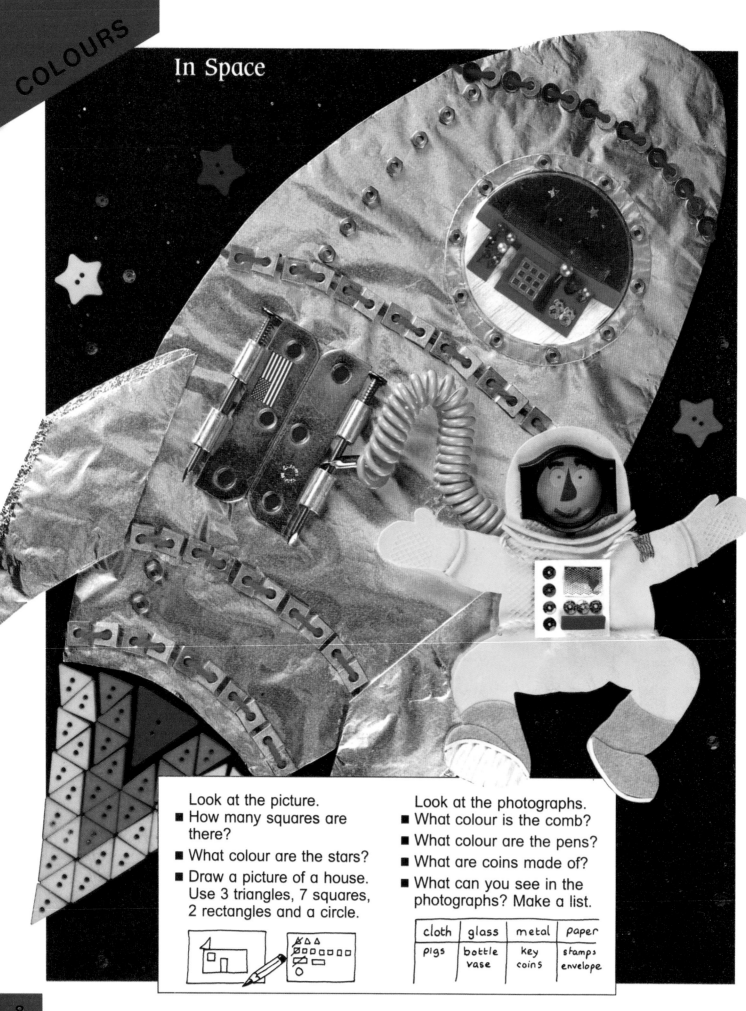

Look at the picture.
- How many squares are there?
- What colour are the stars?
- Draw a picture of a house. Use 3 triangles, 7 squares, 2 rectangles and a circle.

Look at the photographs.
- What colour is the comb?
- What colour are the pens?
- What are coins made of?
- What can you see in the photographs? Make a list.

cloth	glass	metal	paper
pigs	bottle vase	key coins	stamps envelope

COLOURS

MATERIALS

 black

 blue

 brown

 gold

 green

 grey

 orange

 pink

 purple

 red

 silver

 white

 yellow

 cloth

 glass

 metal

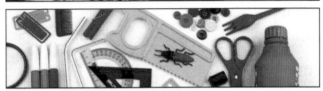 paper

 plastic

 rubber

 wood

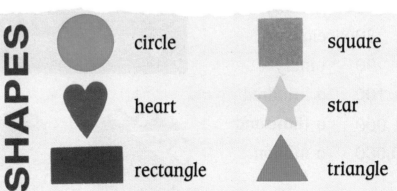 wool

SHAPES

circle

square

heart

star

rectangle

triangle

COLOURS

0	nought/zero
1	one
2	two
3	three
4	four
5	five
6	six
7	seven
8	eight
9	nine
10	ten
11	eleven
12	twelve
13	thirteen
14	fourteen
15	fifteen
16	sixteen
17	seventeen
18	eighteen
19	nineteen
20	twenty
30	thirty
40	forty
50	fifty
60	sixty
70	seventy
80	eighty
90	ninety
100	a hundred
1,000	a thousand
1,000,000	a million

How many?

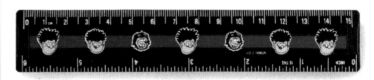

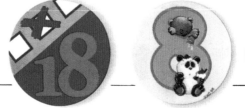

 badge

 ball

 calculator

 car

 clock

 dice

 domino

 playing card

 ruler

FRACTIONS

$\frac{1}{2}$ half

$\frac{1}{4}$ quarter

- Find 7 animals in the photograph.
- Find these numbers in the photograph.
  18 57 15 300
- What numbers are on the badges?
- Count from 1 to 10 in English. Then count backwards from 10 to 1.
- How many cars are there?
  How many rulers?
  How many dice?
  Make a chart.

1	clock
2	calculators

A Day at School

- Find 9 rats in the picture.
- How many pupils can you see in the language laboratory?
- Write the names of the rooms in alphabetical order.
- What is in your bag? Draw pictures and write the words.

My bag
a pencil case
pencils

ROOMS

1 library
2 cloakroom
3 toilet
4 hall
5 language laboratory
6 science laboratory
7 staff room
8 gymnasium/gym
9 office
10 classroom
11 playground

bag

crayons

notebook

pen

pencil

pencil case

pencil sharpener

rubber

ruler

TIMETABLE – CLASS 13

	9·00 10·00	10·00 10·30	10·30 11·30	11·30 12·30	12·30 14·00	14·00 15·30
MON	Maths	B R E A K	English	L U N C H	Geography	Physical Education
TUES	Science		History		Music	Art
WED	Geography		Maths		History	English

13

In the Classroom

- Look at the words on page 15. Find each thing in the picture.
- Look at the picture. Work with a friend. Give instructions. e.g. *Point to the scissors. Point to the calculator.*
- Guess these words.

  ca _ _ _ _ _ _ _ _

  b _ _

  s _ _ _ _

  Now write the words in alphabetical order.

bell   file

bin   glue

blackboard   light

board rubber   paintbrush

bookcase   paper

box   paperclip

calculator   plant

cassette   poster

chair   pupils

chalk   scales

clock   scissors

compass   shelf

computer   stapler

cupboard   sticky tape

desk   string

drawer   tape

drawing   teacher

drawing pin   video

easel   whiteboard

Puppets and Masks

- Find 6 words beginning with the letter **f**.
- Look at the puppets and masks.
  Count the ears. Count the eyes. Count the teeth.
- Which mask has got long eyebrows?
- Which mask has got the biggest ears?
- Write these words in alphabetical order:
  beard   body   back   bottom   bald
- Draw a puppet or mask with a
  long nose, big eyes and curly hair.
  Label your picture.

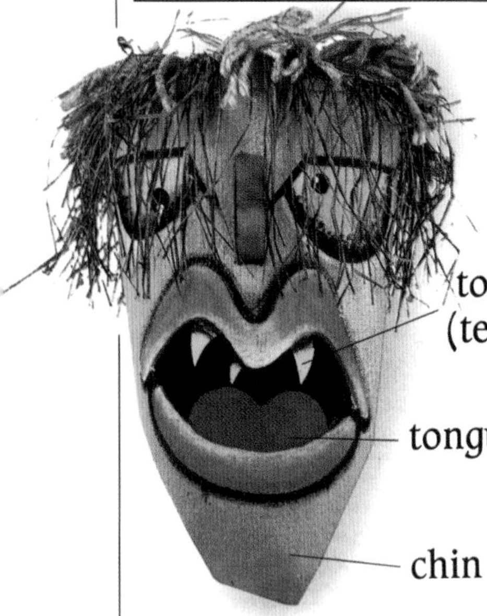

face —

head

back

elbow

body

bottom

tooth
(teeth)

tongue

chin

hair

eyebrow

freckle

beard

stomach

knee

leg

ankle

foot (feet)

16

eyelash

cheek

lip

scar

eye

mouth

neck

shoulder

chest

arm

thumb

finger

forehead

ear

nose

hand

moustache

toe

HAIR

blonde

bald

dark

curly

fair

straight

ginger

The Monster Family

grandparents

grandfather/
grandad

granddaughter

grandmother/
grandma

granddaughter

parents

father/
dad

daughter

mother/
mum

daughter

brothers

sister

aunts/
aunties

niece

uncles

niece

cousin

cousin

grandparents

grandfather

grandson

grandmother

grandson

parents

father

son

mother

son

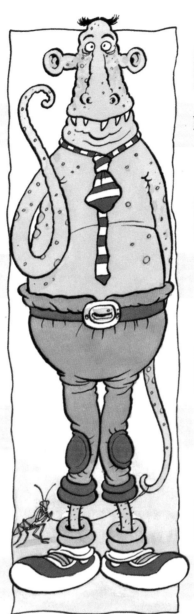

wife

husband

sons

father

daughter

father

nephew

uncle

children

PEOPLE

children

 baby

 boy

 girl

adults

man

 woman

- How many different monsters are there?
- Rearrange the letters to make words.

ecien	phenwe
clune	ieuatn
itsesr	oretbhr
heomtr	rehfta

- The purple monster is called Plum. Give the other monsters a name.
  How many cousins has Plum got?
  Who is Plum's grandmother?
  Write some more questions.

- Find 8 different words with 6 letters.
- Make a poster of yourself and your family. Use photos or draw pictures. Label the pictures.

bikini

 boots

 bra

 cardigan

 coat

 dress

 dressing gown

 dungarees

 gloves

 hat

 jacket

 jeans

 jumper/sweater

 knickers

 nightie

 pyjamas

 scarf

 shirt

 shoes

 shorts

 skirt

 slippers

The Campsite

■ Find these things in the picture.

What are they called in English?

■ Work with a friend. Ask some questions about the picture.
e.g. Who's wearing a red dress?
Who's wearing dungarees?

 socks

 sweatshirt

 swimming costume

 swimming trunks

tie

tights

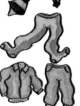 tracksuit

 trainers

 trousers

 t-shirt

 underpants

uniform

 vest

JEWELLERY

 bracelet

earrings

necklace

ring

 belt

button

glasses

hair slide

pocket

ribbon

shoelace

Animals of the World

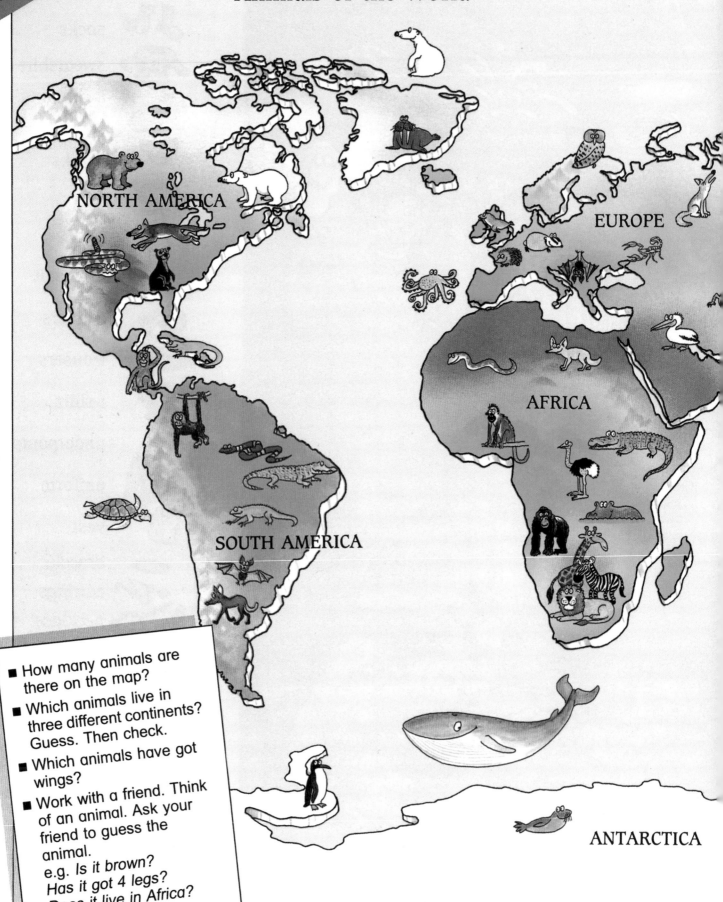

- How many animals are there on the map?
- Which animals live in three different continents? Guess. Then check.
- Which animals have got wings?
- Work with a friend. Think of an animal. Ask your friend to guess the animal.
  e.g. Is it brown?
  Has it got 4 legs?
  Does it live in Africa?

North

West — East

South

	AFRICA	AMERICA	ANTARCTICA	ASIA	AUSTRALASIA	EUROPE
bat	●	●		●	●	●
bear		●		●		●
camel	●			●		
crocodile	●	●			●	
dolphin	●	●			●	●
elephant	●			●		
fox	●	●				●
giraffe	●					
gorilla	●					
hedgehog	●					●
hippopotamus	●					
kangaroo					●	
lion	●			●		
lizard	●	●			●	●
monkey	●	●			●	
octopus	●	●			●	●
ostrich	●					
owl	●	●			●	●
panda				●		
pelican	●	●			●	●
penguin	●	●	●		●	
rhinoceros	●			●		
seal	●	●	●		●	●
shark	●	●			●	●
snake	●	●			●	●
tiger				●		
turtle	●	●			●	●
whale	●	●	●		●	●
wolf	●	●				●
zebra	●					

23

Pets

1	budgie	6	frog	11	parrot
2	canary	7	guinea pig	12	puppy
3	cat	8	hamster	13	rabbit
4	dog	9	kitten	14	rat
5	fish	10	mouse	15	tortoise

- How many mice are there in th[e] pet shop?
- Find these things in the pet shop:

  a basket   **a fish tank**
  a cage   **a kennel**

Farm Animals

How many birds are there on the farm and in the pet shop?

How many chicks are there on the farm?

What is a young cow called?

What colour is the pig?

1	bull	6	donkey	11	horse
2	calf	7	duck	12	lamb
3	chick	8	goat	13	pig
4	cockerel	9	goose	14	piglet
5	cow	10	hen	15	sheep

Fruit and Vegetables

- Find 10 words on this page with 6 letters.
- How many green vegetables are there?
- Work with a friend. Describe a fruit or vegetable.
  e.g. *It's a long orange vegetable.*
  Ask your friend to guess the name.

- Ask your friends:
  Do you like potatoes?
  Do you like apples?
  What's your favourite fruit?
  What's your favourite vegetable?
- Make a list of fruit and vegetables.

fruit	vegetables
apple apricot	asparagus

apple

apricot

beans

cauliflower

celery

cherries

cucumber

grapefruit

grapes

leek

melon

mushroom

onion

orange

papaya

plum

potato

raspberry

spinach

sprouts

asparagus

aubergine

avocado

banana

beetroot

broccoli

cabbage

carrot

coconut

corn

courgette

lemon

lettuce

lime

mango

peach

pear

peas

pepper

pineapple

strawberry

tomato

turnip

watermelon

A Party

birthday cake

biscuit

cheeseburger

chocolate

cola

crisps

doughnut

hamburger

hot dog

- How many glasses are there on the table?
- Find 8 things beginning with the letter **s**.
- Close the dictionary. Can you remember what is on the table?
- What are these?

- What did you eat and drink yesterday? Make a list.

breakfast	lunch	dinner	supper
orange juice cornflakes	salad	chicken rice	toast

DRINKS ON THE TABLE

 beer

 coffee

 fruit juice

 milk

 tea

 water

 wine

 ketchup

 mustard

 pepper

 salt

 sugar

 vinegar

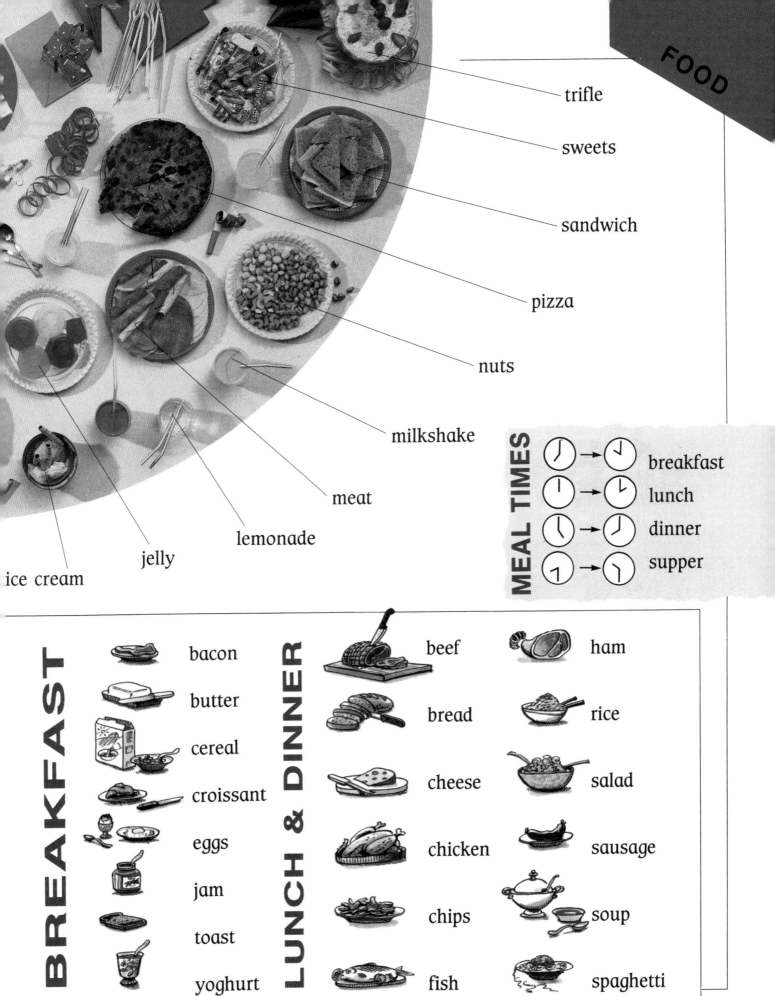

trifle

sweets

sandwich

pizza

nuts

milkshake

meat

lemonade

jelly

ice cream

MEAL TIMES

breakfast

lunch

dinner

supper

BREAKFAST

bacon

butter

cereal

croissant

eggs

jam

toast

yoghurt

LUNCH & DINNER

beef

bread

cheese

chicken

chips

fish

ham

rice

salad

sausage

soup

spaghetti

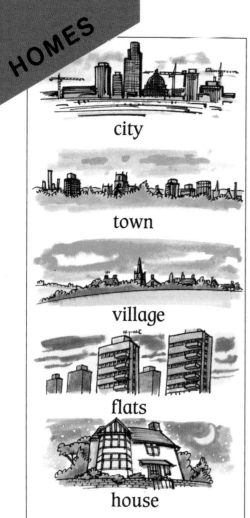

city

town

village

flats

house

bathroom

OUTSIDE

1 aerial
2 balcony
3 chimney
4 garage
5 garden
6 roof

 bath

 bed

 blanket

 carpet

 curtain

 duvet

 lamp

 mirror

 picture

 pillow

 plug

 rug

bedroom

 sheets

 shower

 soap

 tap

 toilet

 toilet paper

 toothbrush

 toothpaste

 towel

 vase

 wardrobe

 washbasin

- Find 10 coins in the picture.
- Find 5 red things in the picture.
- Translate these words:

  bath blanket curtain bed carpet

  Write them in alphabetical order in your language.
- Which things are in the bedroom and which things are in the bathroom? Make a list.

bedroom	bathroom
bed blanket	bath

HOMES

Downstairs

stairs

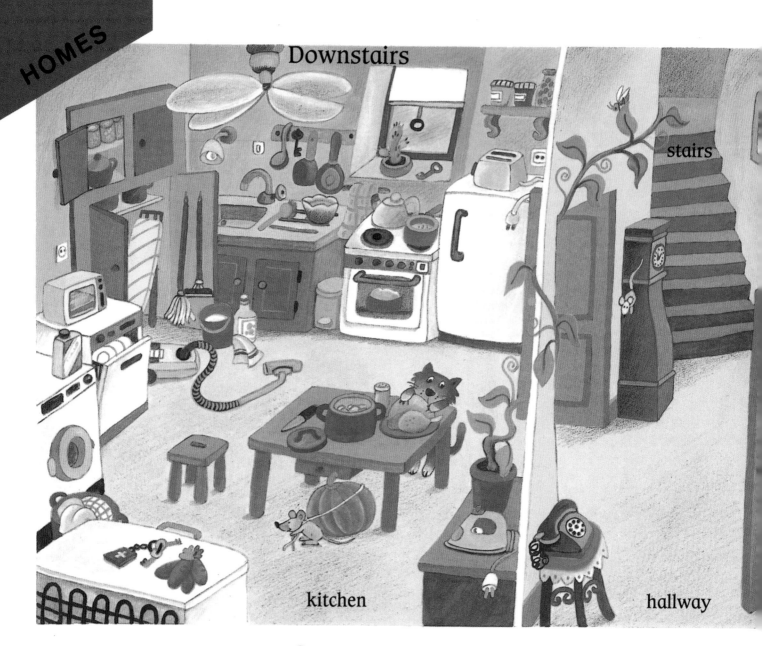

kitchen

hallway

- Find 10 keys in the picture.
- Find 3 things in the kitchen beginning with the letter **c**.
- Find 3 things in the living room beginning with the letter **p**.
- Close your book. Can you remember what is in the living room?
- What colour is the kettle?
- Write the name of 5 things that are in the living room and in the kitchen too.

 armchair

 blind

 bottle

 cooker

 cushion

 dishwasher

 fan

 freezer

 fridge

 iron

 ironing board

 jar

living/dining room

ON THE TABLE

bowl

cup

fork

glass

knife

mug

plate

saucer

spoon

tablecloth

teapot

 kettle

 microwave

 mop

 oven

 pan

 plug

 sewing machine

 sink

 sofa/settee

 stereo

 stool

 switch

 telephone

 television/TV

 toaster

 tray

 vacuum cleaner

 washing machine

Air, Land and Sea

- How many animals are there in the picture?
- Find these things in the picture:
  a helmet
  a petrol pump
  a runway
  a satellite
- Look at the words on page 35. Work with a friend. Ask some questions about spelling. e.g. *How do you spell plane?*
  Check your friend's answers.

 aeroplane/plane

 airship

 ambulance

 balloon

 barge

 bicycle/bike

 boat

 bus

 canoe

 car

 caravan

 coach

 ferry

 fire engine

 hang glider

 helicopter

 hovercraft

 lorry/truck

 minibus

 motorbike

 parachute

 police car

 pram

 pushchair

 rocket

 roller skates

 scooter

 ship

 skateboard

 space ship

 space shuttle

 speedboat

 submarine

 tank

 train

 tram

 tricycle

 van

 wheelchair

 yacht

Ruby's Room

TOYS

 ball
 bat
 bricks
 cards
 clown
 computer game
 doll
 doll's house
 games
 gun
 jigsaw puzzle
 paints
 robot
 skipping rope
 soft toys
 teddy
 train set
 walkie-talkies

PERSONAL THINGS

 books
 camera
 comb
 diary
 football boots
 hairbrush
 hairdryer
 handbag
headphones

 make-up
 money
 money box
 personal stereo
 purse
 sports bag
 torch
 typewriter
 watch

HOBBIES

THINGS TO COLLECT

 autographs
 badges
 coins
comics
 medals
 models
 photographs
 postcards
 stamps

- Find 8 things in the picture beginning with the letter **c**.
- Which of these things is not in the picture?

  a car
  a doll
  a medal
  a purse
  a robot
  a watch

- Connect the words.

  computer   **rope**
  skipping   **puzzle**
  money   **dryer**
  photo   **game**
  jigsaw   **boots**
  hair   **album**
  football   **box**

- Work with a friend. Ask some questions about the picture.
  e.g. Where's the purse?
  What colour's the comb?

37

Music

1	banjo	8	guitar	15	synthesizer
2	cello	9	harp	16	tambourine
3	clarinet	10	maracas	17	triangle
4	cymbals	11	mouth organ	18	trombone
5	double bass	12	piano	19	trumpet
6	drums	13	recorder	20	violin
7	flute	14	saxophone	21	xylophone

- Which instruments do you blow?
- Cover the words on page 3 Can you remember the nam of the instruments? Check your answers and tr again.
- What is the difference betwe a double bass and a cello?

Sport

athletics

baseball

basketball

cricket

football

golf

gymnastics

horse riding

ice skating

judo

skiing

swimming

In which sports do you use these things?

Rearrange the letters and make words.

ktreicc   llabbtaeks
nnstie   lfloaobt

table tennis

tennis

This is a board game for two or more players.

You need:

dice →  ← counters

Rules

1. Put your counters on START.

2. Throw the dice. Move your counter.

3. When you land on a square, do the action, e.g. cough if you land on square 4.

4. If you do the action wrongly, miss a turn.

5. The first player to reach FINISH is the winner.

- Find these things in the pictures:

a bottle	**a pencil**
a lamp	**a stool**

- Say this rhyme and do the actions.

  Point to the ceiling,
  Touch the floor.
  Open the window,
  And close the door.

- What are the boys and girls doing? Make a list.

boys	girls
close	blow
	clap

START

1 blow

2 clap

15 laugh

14 kneel

13 GO BACK 4 SQUARES

16 open

17 pick up

18 point

31 touch

30 GO FORWARD 6 SQUARES

29 stand up

32 turn off

33 turn on

34 walk

close

cough

crawl

cry

dance

jump

hop

fall

drop

draw

read

run

MISS A TURN

scratch

scream

smile

sit down

sing

shout

shake

wave

whisper

whistle

write

FINISH

In the Playground

1	argue	13	fight	25	measure
2	bite	14	fish	26	paint
3	bounce	15	fly	27	pull
4	build	16	give	28	push
5	buy	17	hide	29	ride
6	carry	18	hit	30	skate
7	catch	19	hug	31	ski
8	climb	20	juggle	32	skip
9	copy	21	kick	33	swim
10	dig	22	kiss	34	take
11	dive	23	knock	35	tear
12	drive	24	lift	36	throw

- How many children are there in the playground?
  How many boys? How many girls?
- What are they doing?

He's throwing a ball. *She's juggling.* *They're arguing.*

Point to the children in the picture. Ask your friend:
What's he doing?
What's she doing?

- Pick a number from 1 to 36. Say the number.
  Ask your friend to mime the action.
- There are five letters in the picture.
  Find the letters and make a word.
- Ask your friends:
  Can you swim? *Can you skate?*
  Can you ski? *Can you juggle?*
  Draw a graph.

In the Home

break

brush

clean

dream

drink

dry

go to bed

have a bath

have a shower

mend

peel

pour

stretch

sweep

take off

wash

wash up

watch

comb

cook

cut

eat

get dressed

get up

iron

knit

listen

put on

sew

sleep

tie

wake up

weigh

yawn

■ Find these things in the pictures:

**an apple   an iron
a cake   a towel**

■ All of these words are verbs. Which words are also nouns?

**comb drink eat iron
listen**

■ Mime one of the actions. Ask a friend to guess what you are doing.
e.g. *Are you washing your hands?*

The Town

How many animals are the in the picture?

Find these things in the picture:
- **a bottle**
- **a guitar**
- **a pan**
- **a spaceship**

BUILDINGS

1	airport	7	factory
2	bank	8	hospital
3	cafe	9	hotel
4	car park	10	market
5	church	11	mosque
6	cinema	12	museum

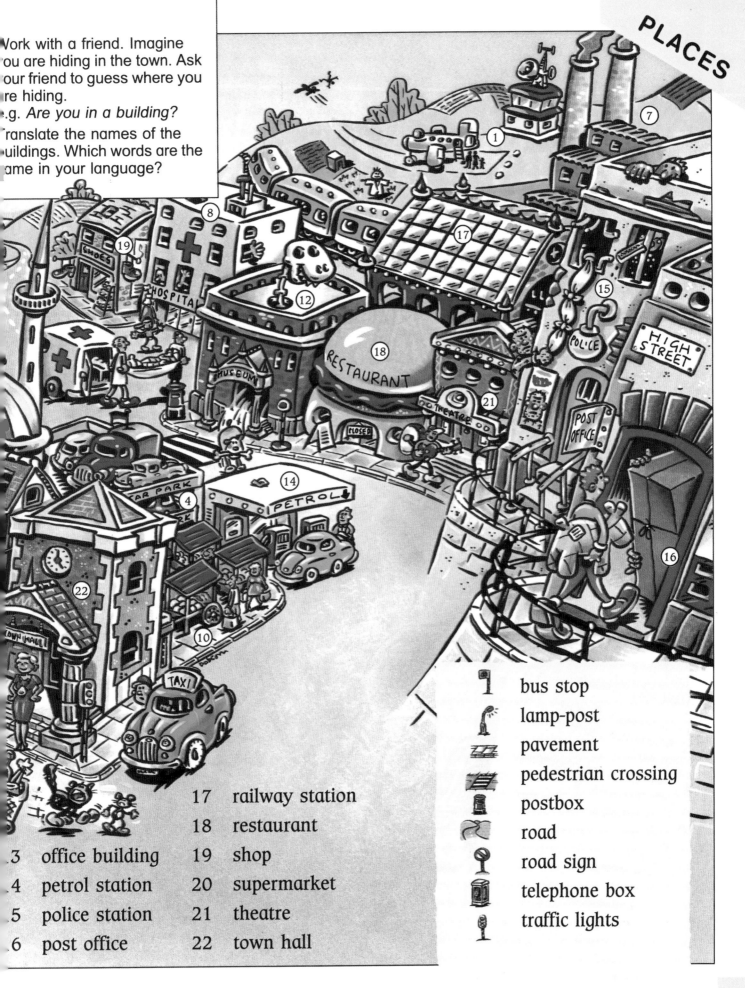

Work with a friend. Imagine you are hiding in the town. Ask your friend to guess where you are hiding.

e.g. *Are you in a building?*

Translate the names of the buildings. Which words are the same in your language?

17	railway station
18	restaurant
13	office building	19	shop
14	petrol station	20	supermarket
15	police station	21	theatre
16	post office	22	town hall

- bus stop
- lamp-post
- pavement
- pedestrian crossing
- postbox
- road
- road sign
- telephone box
- traffic lights

The Countryside

- How many different animals are there in the picture?
- Find 8 things beginning with the letter **s**.
- Find these things in the picture:

  a fire
  a hammock
  a nest
  a scarecrow
  a stone

- What is the difference between a mountain and a hill?

1	bridge	7	hill	13	river
2	canal	8	lake	14	rubbish tip
3	cave	9	motorway	15	stream
4	field	10	mountain	16	tunnel
5	forest	11	power station	17	valley
6	grass	12	reservoir	18	waterfall

barn

bush

farmhouse

fence

fire

gate

hammock

haystack

leaves

litter

nest

picnic

pylon

rucksack

scarecrow

signpost

smoke

stick

stone

tent

tractor

tree

The Seaside

sky

cliff

sea

beach

bucket

crab

deckchair

feather

island

lighthouse

pebbles

rocks

sand

sand castle

seaweed

shells

spade

starfish

sunglasses

suntan lotion

surfboard

waves

- Find these things in the pictures:

  flowers   **a slide**
  goggles   **a swing**

- Find two things that are in all three pictures.

- Find a picture of the seaside or a swimming pool in a magazine. Stick the picture on a sheet of paper. Label the picture.

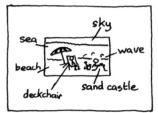

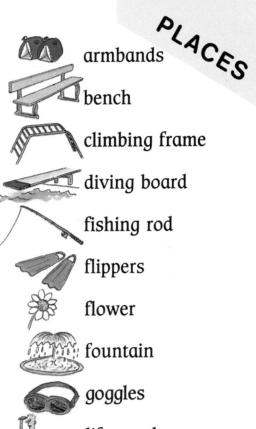PLACES

The Park

The Swimming Pool

armbands

bench

climbing frame

diving board

fishing rod

flippers

flower

fountain

goggles

lifeguard

litter bin

pond

rope

roundabout

rubber ring

sandpit

seesaw

slide

snorkel

swing

water

wheelbarrow

51

When I grow up...

1 actor   2 actress   3 artist   4 bank clerk   5 builder

10 doctor   11 electrician   12 fireman

15 nurse   16 pilot   17 plumber

21 secretary   22 shop assistant   23 singer

■ What are these things called in English? Who uses them?

6   bus driver

7   chef

8   dancer

9   dentist

13   hairdresser

14   mechanic

18   policewoman

19   postman

20   scientist

Rearrange the letters to make words.

irbleud   crsaeyetr
etv   mlbrpue

Work with a friend.
Point to a boy or a girl in the picture. Ask your friend:
What does he want to be?
What does she want to be?
What do you want to be?
Ask your friends.

24   vet

25   waiter

26   waitress

Once upon a time...

- Find 4 things beginning with the letter **c**.
- How many **crowns** are there in the picture?
- Are these sentences true or false?
  - **The giant is holding an axe.**
  - **The skeleton is flying on the broomstick.**
  - **The dragon is red.**
  - **The pirate is wearing a crown.**

STORYBOOK CHARACTERS

1 alien
2 dragon
3 fairy
4 genie
5 ghost
6 giant
7 king
8 mermaid
9 monster
10 pirate
11 prince
12 princess
13 queen
14 skeleton
15 vampire
16 witch
17 wizard

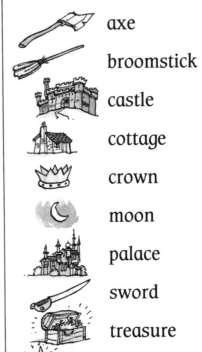

axe
broomstick
castle
cottage
crown
moon
palace
sword
treasure
wand

The Calendar

Monday	**1** first	**8** eighth	**15** fifteenth	**22** twenty-second	**29** twenty-ninth
Tuesday	**2** second	**9** ninth	**16** sixteenth	**23** twenty-third	**30** thirtieth
Wednesday	**3** third	**10** tenth	**17** seventeenth	**24** twenty-fourth	**31** thirty-first
Thursday	**4** fourth	**11** eleventh	**18** eighteenth	**25** twenty-fifth	
Friday	**5** fifth	**12** twelfth	**19** nineteenth	**26** twenty-sixth	
Saturday	**6** sixth	**13** thirteenth	**20** twentieth	**27** twenty-seventh	
Sunday	**7** seventh	**14** fourteenth	**21** twenty-first	**28** twenty-eighth	

weekend

1st first   **2**nd second   **3**rd third   **4**th fourth

MONTHS

January
February
March
April
May
June
July
August
September
October
November
December

Mon	1	8	15	22	29
Tue	2	9	16	23	30
Wed	3	10	17	24	31
Thur	4	11	18	25	
Fri	5	12	19	26	
Sat	6	13	20	27	
Sun	7	14	21	28	

WHAT'S THE TIME?

← quarter to...

→ quarter past...

↓ half past...

↑ ...o'clock

p.m. ↑↑ midday

a.m. ↑↑ midnight

60 seconds = 1 minute
60 minutes = 1 hour
24 hours = 1 day
7 days = 1 week
52 weeks = 1 year

 morning
06.00 – 12.00

 afternoon
12.00 – 18.00

evening
18.00 – 24.00

night
24.00 – 06.00

■ What's the time?

■ Write the days of the week in alphabetical order.
■ Say the months in English backwards.
■ What is the date today?
■ What was the date yesterday?
■ When is your birthday? Ask your friends. Draw a graph.

January	▨▨▨				
February	▨▨▨				
March	▨				

SEASONS

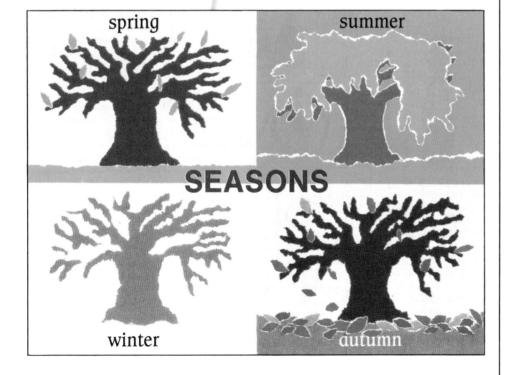

spring   summer

winter   autumn

Beautiful or ugly?

- Find 5 words beginning with the letter **c**.
- Say a word. Ask your friend to say the opposite.
- Which words mean the same?

  closed   **big**
  difficult   **dear**
  expensive   **hard**
  large   **little**
  loud   **noisy**
  small   **shut**

- Which words describe each picture?

  cold   **long**
  fat   **sharp**
  light

beautiful / ugly

big/large / little/small

day / night

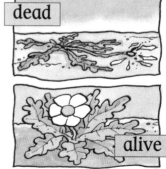

dead / alive

front / back

good / bad

happy / sad

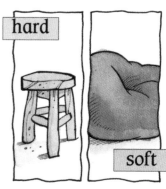

hard / soft

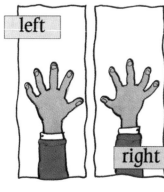

left / right

long / short

new / old

noisy/loud / quiet

ROAR!

Eek!

rough / smooth

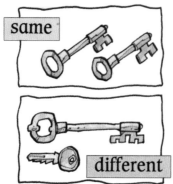

same / different

short / tall

strong / weak

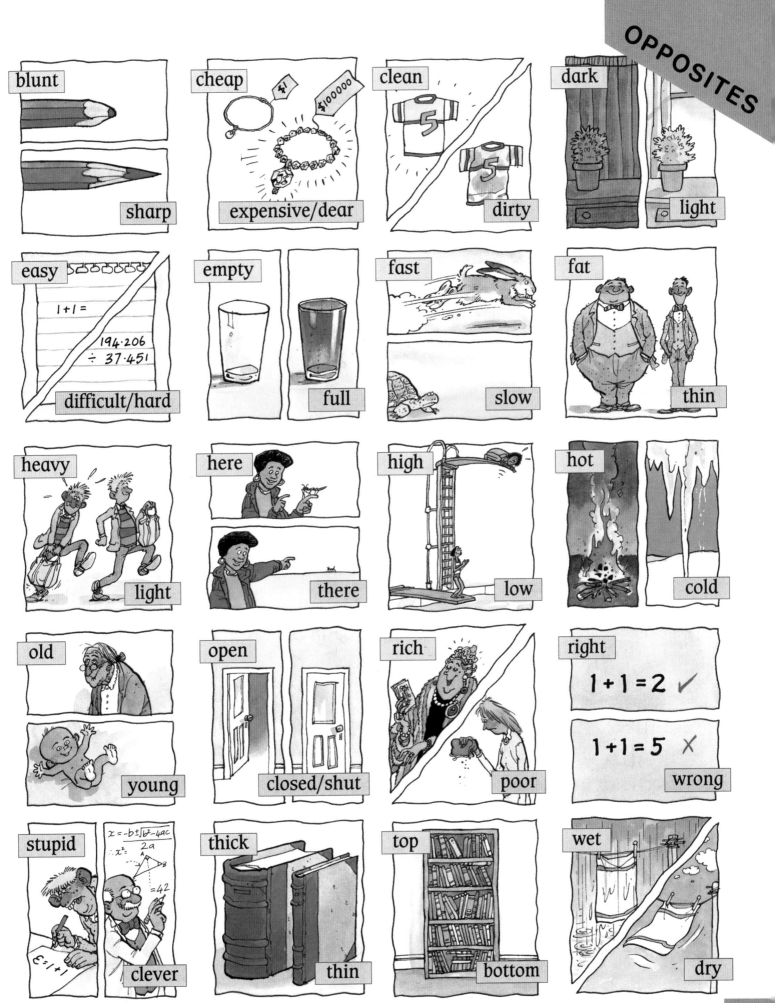

blunt — sharp

cheap — expensive/dear

clean — dirty

dark — light

easy — difficult/hard

empty — full

fast — slow

fat — thin

heavy — light

here — there

high — low

hot — cold

old — young

open — closed/shut

rich — poor

right — wrong

stupid — clever

thick — thin

top — bottom

wet — dry

Where is it?

above

The rat is **above** the hat.

duck   hen

The birds are **above** the words.

behind

The fox is **behind** the rocks.

The frog is sitting **behind** the dog.

between

The fox is **between** the rocks.

down

The bears are walking **down** the stairs.

in

There is a mouse **in** the house.

The fish is **in** the dish.

in front of

The fox is **in front of** the rocks.

The frog is sitting **in front of** the dog.

into

The slug is crawling **into** the jug.

near

The cat is **near** the rat.

Where are the frogs?

next to/by

The rat is **next to** the hat.

on

The cat is **on** the mat.

There are two pictures **on** the wall, one is big and one is small.

out of

There's a witch on a broom flying **out of** the room.

over

There's a snake crawling **over** the cake.

under

There is a hare **under** the chair.

duck   hen

The words are **under** the birds.

up

The bears are walking **up** the stairs.

POSITIONS

- Find 3 things beginning with the letter **f.**
- What are these?

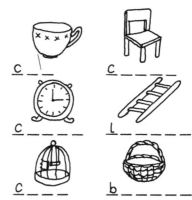

c _ _   c _ _ _ _

c _ _ _ _   L _ _ _ _ _

c _ _ _   b _ _ _ _ _

- Work with a friend. Ask some questions about the frogs.
  e.g. *Where's the green frog?*
  Where's the blue frog?
  Is the red frog under the chair?

- **Fish** rhymes with **dish.**
  Connect the words that rhyme.

  birds   hair
  chair   box
  frog   words
  rat   dog
  rocks   hat

- Find 8 words in the puzzle.

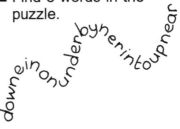

downeinonunderbyherintoupnear

61

What's the weather like?

It's cloudy. It's warm.

It's foggy.

It's raining. It's wet.

It's snowing. It's cold.

It's sunny. It's hot.

It's windy.

cloud

fog

ice

lightning

puddle

rain

snow

sun

thunder

- Find these things in the pictures:

  a bucket
  a kite
  a glove
  sunglasses

- Copy the puzzle. Write the words.

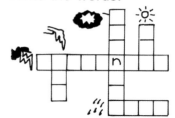

62

Insects and small creatures

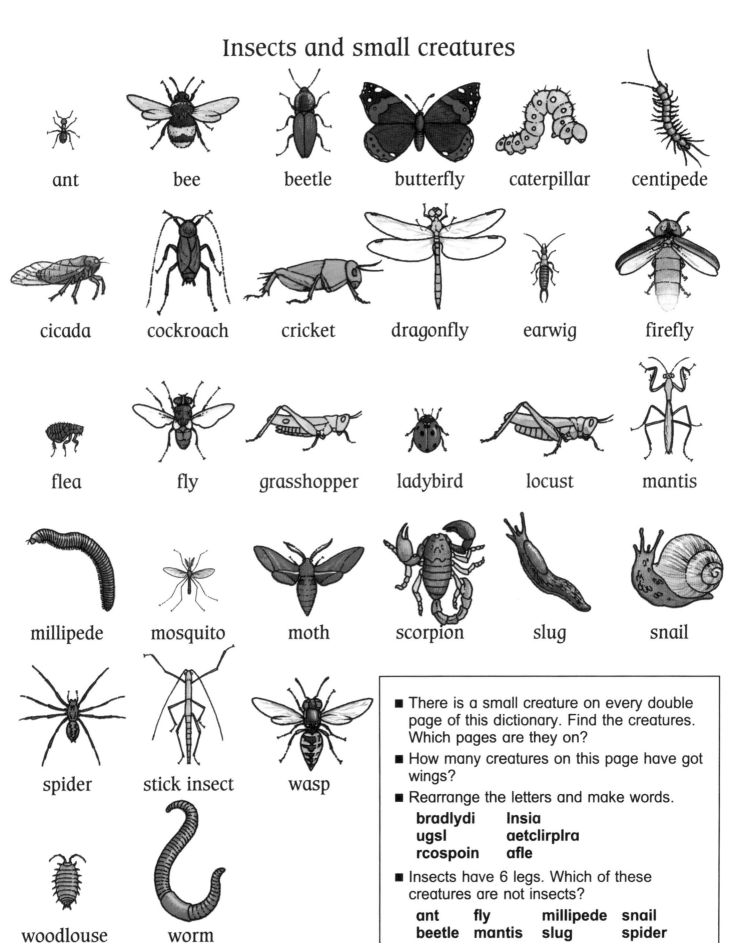

ant

bee

beetle

butterfly

caterpillar

centipede

cicada

cockroach

cricket

dragonfly

earwig

firefly

flea

fly

grasshopper

ladybird

locust

mantis

millipede

mosquito

moth

scorpion

slug

snail

spider

stick insect

wasp

woodlouse

worm

- There is a small creature on every double page of this dictionary. Find the creatures. Which pages are they on?
- How many creatures on this page have got wings?
- Rearrange the letters and make words.

   bradlydi   **lnsia**
   ugsl   **aetclrplra**
   rcospoin   **afle**

- Insects have 6 legs. Which of these creatures are not insects?

   ant   **fly**   **millipede**   **snail**
   beetle   **mantis**   **slug**   **spider**

63

Flags, Countries and Nationalities

 Argentina / Argentinian

 Australia / Australian

 Austria / Austrian

 Belgium / Belgian

 Brazil / Brazilian

 Canada / Canadian

 Chile / Chilean

 Denmark / Danish

 Eire / Irish

 Finland / Finnish

 France / French

 Germany / German

Greece / Greek

 India / Indian

 Italy / Italian

 Japan / Japanese

 Mexico / Mexican

 The Netherlands / Dutch

 New Zealand / New Zealander

 Norway / Norwegian

 Peru / Peruvian

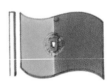 Portugal / Portuguese

 Spain / Spanish

 Sweden / Swedish

 Switzerland / Swiss

 Turkey / Turkish

 The U.K. / British

 The U.S.A. / American

 Venezuela / Venezuelan

- There is a flag on every double page of this dictionary. Find the flags. Which pages are they on?
- How many flags are red, white and blue?
- Which flag is blue and yellow?
- How many stars are there on the Australian flag?
- Which flags are these?

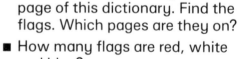

64

AaBbCcDdEeFfGgHhIiJjKkLlMm

Wordlist

The following pages contain an alphabetical list of all the words in the dictionary. Next to each word is the number of the page on which the word appears.

NnOoPpQqRrSsTtUuVvWwXxYyZz

a

above 60

actor 52

actress 52

adult 19

aerial 30

aeroplane 35

Africa 23

afternoon 57

airport 46

airship 35

alien 55

alive 58

ALPHABET 6-7

ambulance 35

America 23

American 64

ANIMALS 22-25

ankle 16

ant 63

Antarctica 23

apple 26

apricot 26

April 57

Argentina 64

Argentinian 64

argue 43

arm 17

armband 51

armchair 32

art 13

artist 52

Asia 23

asparagus 27

astronaut 7

athletics 39

aubergine 27

August 57

aunt 18

aunty (aunties) 18

Australasia 23

Australia 64

Australian 64

Austria 64

Austrian 64

autograph 37

autumn 57

avocado 27

axe 55

b

baby 19

back 16, 58

bacon 29

bad 58

badge 11, 37

bag 13

balcony 30

bald 17

ball 11, 37

balloon 7, 35

banana 27

banjo 38

bank 46

bank clerk 52

barge 35

barn 49

baseball 39

basketball 39

bat 23, 37

bath 30

bathroom 30

beach 50

bean 26

bear 23

beard 16

beautiful 58

bed 30

bedroom 31

bee 63

beef 29

beer 28

beetle 63

beetroot 27

behind 60

Belgian 64

Belgium 64

bell 15

belt 21

bench 51

between 60

bicycle 35

big 58

bike 35

bikini 20

bin 15

birthday cake 28

biscuit 28

bite 43

black 9

blackboard 15

blanket 30

blind 32

blonde 17

blow 40

blue 9

blunt 59

board game 40

board rubber 15

boat 35

BODY 16-17

book 37

bookcase 15

boot 20

bottle 32

bottom 16, 59

bounce 43

bowl 33

box 15

boy 19

bra 20

bracelet 21

Brazil 64

Brazilian 64

bread 29

break 13, 44

breakfast 29

brick 37

bridge 49

British 64

broccoli 27

broom 61

broomstick 55

brother 18

brown 9

brush 7, 44

bucket 50

budgie 24

build 43

builder 52

building 46

bull 25

bus 35

bus driver 53

bush 49

bus stop 47

butter 29

butterfly 63

button 21

buy 43

by 61

C

cabbage 27

cafe 46

cage 7

calculator 11, 15

calendar 56

calf 25

camel 23

camera 37

campsite 20

Canada 64

Canadian 64

canal 49

canary 24

candle 7

canoe 35

capital letter 7

car 11, 35

caravan 35

car park 46

card 37

cardigan 20

carpet 30

67

carrot 27

carry 43

cassette 15

castle 55

cat 24

catch 43

caterpillar 63

cauliflower 26

cave 49

ceiling 14

celery 26

cello 38

centipede 63

cereal 29

chair 15

chalk 15

character 55

cheap 59

cheek 17

cheese 29

cheeseburger 28

chef 53

cherry (cherries) 26

chest 17

chick 25

chicken 29

child (children) 19

Chile 64

Chilean 64

chimney 30

chin 16

chip 29

chocolate 28

church 46

cicada 63

cinema 46

circle 9

circus 36

city 30

clap 40

clarinet 38

class 13

classroom 12

clean 44, 59

clever 59

cliff 50

climb 43

climbing frame 51

cloakroom 12

clock 11, 15

close 41

closed 59

cloth 9

CLOTHES 20-21

cloud 62

cloudy 62

clown 37

coach 35

coat 20

cobweb 7

cockerel 25

cockroach 63

coconut 27

coffee 28

coin 37

cola 28

cold 59, 62

COLOURS 8-9

comb 37, 45

comic 37

comma 7

compass 15

computer 15

computer game 37

cook 45

cooker 32

copy 43

corn 27

cottage 55

cough 41

counter 40

country 64

countryside 48

courgette 27

cousin 18

cow 25

crab 50

crawl 41

crayon 13

creature 63

cricket 39, 63

crisp 28

crocodile 23

croissant 29

crown 55

cry 41

cucumber 26

cup 33

cupboard 15

curly 17

curtain 30

cushion 32

cut 45

cymbal 38

d

dad 18

dance 41

dancer 53

Danish 64

dark 17, 59

daughter 18

day 58

dead 58

dear 59

December 57

deckchair 50

Denmark 64

dentist 53

desk 15

diary 37

dice 11, 40

different 58

difficult 59

dig 43

dining room 33

dinner 29

dinosaur 7

dirty 59

dish 60

dishwasher 32

dive 43

diving board 51

doctor 52

dog 24

doll 37

doll's house 37

dolphin 23

domino 11

donkey 25

door 15

double bass 38

doughnut 28

down 60

downstairs 32

dragon 55

dragonfly 63

draw 41

drawer 15

drawing 15

drawing pin 15

dream 44

dress 20

dressing gown 20

drink 28, 44

drive 43

drop 41

drum 38

dry 44, 59

duck 25

dungarees 20

dustbin 7

Dutch 64

duvet 30

e

ear 17

earring 21

earwig 63

easel 15

east 23

easy 59

eat 45

egg 29

eight 10

eighteen 10

eighty 10

Eire 64

elbow 16
electrician 52
elephant 23
eleven 10
empty 59
English 13
entrance 12
envelope 7
Europe 23
evening 57
exit 46
expensive 59
eye 17
eyebrow 16
eyelash 17

face 16
factory 46
fair 17
fairy 55
fall 41
FAMILY 18-19
fan 32
farm 25
farmhouse 49
fast 59

fat 59
father 18
feather 50
February 57
fence 49
ferry 35
field 49
fifteen 10
fifty 10
fight 43
file 15
film 46
finger 17
finish 41
Finland 64
Finnish 64
fire 49
fire engine 35
firefly 63
fireman 52
firework 7
first 56
fish 24, 29, 43
fishing rod 51
five 10
FLAGS 64, 7
flat 30
flea 63
flipper 51
floor 15
flower 51

flute 38
fly 43, 63
fog 62
foggy 62
FOOD 26-29
foot (feet) 16
football 39
football boot 37
forehead 17
forest 49
fork 33
forty 10
fountain 51
four 10
fourteen 10
fourth 56
fox 23
fraction 11
France 64
freckle 16
freezer 32
French 64
Friday 56
fridge 32
frog 24
front 58
fruit 26
fruit juice 28
full 59
full stop 7

g

game 37

garage 30

garden 30

gate 49

genie 55

geography 13

German 64

Germany 64

get dressed 45

get up 45

ghost 55

giant 55

ginger 17

giraffe 23

girl 19

give 43

glass 9, 33

glasses 21

glove 20

glue 15

go to bed 44

goat 25

goggles 51

gold 9

golf 39

good 58

goose 25

gorilla 23

grandad 18

granddaughter 18

grandfather 18

grandma 18

grandmother 18

grandparent 18

grandson 19

grape 26

grapefruit 26

grass 49

grasshopper 7, 63

Greece 64

Greek 64

green 9

grey 9

guinea pig 24

guitar 38

gun 37

gym 12

gymnasium 12

gymnastics 39

h

hair 16

hairbrush 37

hairdresser 53

hairdryer 37

hair slide 21

half 11

half past 57

hall 12

hallway 32

ham 29

hamburger 28

hammer 7

hammock 49

hamster 24

hand 17

handbag 37

hang glider 35

happy 58

hard 58, 59

hare 61

harp 38

hat 20

have a bath 44

have a shower 44

haystack 49

head 16

headphones 37

heart 9

heavy 59

hedgehog 23

helicopter 35

hen 25

here 59

hide 43

i

j

k

l

ladder 7
ladybird 63
lake 49
lamb 25
lamp 30
lamp-post 47
land 34
language laboratory 12
large 58
laugh 40
leaf (leaves) 49
leek 26
left 58
leg 16
lemon 27
lemonade 29
letter 7
lettuce 27
library 12
lifeguard 51
lift 43
light 15, 59
lighthouse 50
lightning 62
lime 27
lion 23
lip 17

listen 45
litter 49
litter bin 51
little 58
living room 33
lizard 23
lobster 7
locust 63
long 58
lorry 35
loud 58
low 59
lunch 13, 29

m

magnet 7
make-up 37
man 19
mango 27
mantis 63
maracas 38
March 57
market 46
mask 16
mat 61
match 7
material 9

maths 13
May 57
meal 29
measure 43
meat 29
mechanic 53
medal 37
melon 26
mend 44
mermaid 55
metal 9
Mexican 64
Mexico 64
microwave 33
midday 57
midnight 57
milk 28
milkshake 29
million 10
millipede 63
minibus 35
minute 57
mirror 30
model 37
Monday 56
money 37
money box 37
monkey 23
monster 18, 55
month 57
moon 55

O

n

p

q

quarter 11
quarter past 57
quarter to 57
queen 7, 55
question mark 7
quiet 58

r

rabbit 24
railway station 47
rain 62
rainbow 7
raspberry 26
rat 24
read 41
recorder 38
rectangle 9
red 9
reservoir 49
restaurant 47
rhinoceros 23
ribbon 21
rice 29

rich 59
ride 43
right 58, 59
ring 21
river 49
road 47
road sign 47
robot 37
rock 50
rocket 35
roller skate 35
roof 30
room 12, 36
rope 7, 51
rough 58
roundabout 51
rubber 9, 13
rubber ring 51
rubbish tip 49
rucksack 49
rug 30
ruler 11, 13
run 41

s

sad 58
salad 29

salt 28
same 58
sand 50
sand castle 50
sandpit 51
sandwich 29
Saturday 56
saucer 33
sausage 29
saxophone 38
scales 15
scar 17
scarecrow 49
scarf 20
SCHOOL 12-15
science 13
science laboratory 12
scientist 53
scissors 15
scooter 35
scorpion 63
scratch 41
scream 41
sea 50
seal 23
seaside 50
season 57
seaweed 50
second 56, 57
secretary 52
seesaw 51

September 57

settee 33

seven 10

seventeen 10

seventy 10

sew 45

sewing machine 33

shake 41

shape 9

shark 23

sharp 59

sheep 25

sheet 31

shelf 15

shell 50

ship 35

shirt 20

shoe 20

shoelace 21

shop 47

shop assistant 52

short 58

shorts 20

shoulder 17

shout 41

shower 31

shut 59

signpost 49

silver 9

sing 41

singer 52

sink 33

sister 18

sit down 41

six 10

sixteen 10

sixty 10

skate 43

skateboard 35

skeleton 55

ski 43

skiing 39

skip 43

skipping rope 37

skirt 20

sky 50

sleep 45

slide 51

slipper 20

slow 59

slug 60, 63

small 58

small letter 7

smile 41

smoke 49

smooth 58

snail 63

snake 23

snorkel 51

snow 62

snowman 7

soap 31

sock 21

sofa 33

soft 58

soft toy 37

son 19

soup 29

south 23

space 8

space ship 35

space shuttle 35

spade 50

spaghetti 29

Spain 64

Spanish 64

speedboat 35

spider 63

spinach 26

spoon 33

sport 39

sports bag 37

spring 57

sprout 26

square 9

staff room 12

stairs 32

stamp 37

stand up 40

stapler 15

star 9

starfish 50

start 40

t

u

V

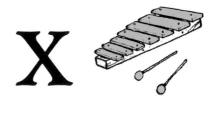
W

X

y

Z